John
"Mr. Canada"

Bill McNe

Contents

Prologue   3
1   The Fishers of Frosty Hollow   7
2   Choosing a Direction   13
3   A National Network for Canada   18
4   The Emerging Broadcaster   23
5   "John Fisher Reports"   31
6   Centennial in the Making   42
7   Centennial Year   49
8   The Final Years   61

The Canadians: A continuing series
General Editor: Robert Read
Designer: Sandi Meland Cherun
Editor: Margaret Woollard

The Author
Cape Breton-born Bill McNeil, a broadcaster with more than thirty years' network radio experience, is the host of the CBC *program "Fresh Air". He is also the author of* Voice of the Pioneer, *a book based on material from his CBC radio network program of the same name, and co-author of* Signing On: The Birth of Radio in Canada.

©1983 Fitzhenry & Whiteside Limited
        195 Allstate Parkway
        Markham, Ontario L3R 4T8

Canadian Cataloguing in Publication Data

McNeil, Bill, 1924-
     John Fisher: "Mr. Canada"

(The Canadians)
Bibliography: p.
ISBN 0-88902-524-X

1. Fisher, John, 1912-1981 - Juvenile literature.
2. Radio broadcasters - Canada - Biography - Juvenile
literature.   3. Canada - Biography - Juvenile
literature.   I. Title.   II. Series.

FC601.F57M46 1983   j971.064'092'4   C83-099286-3
F1034.2.F57M46 1983

Prologue

In 1912, when John Wiggins Fisher was born, the Canadian nation was forty-five years old. In the years since Confederation in 1867, the young Dominion had made great progress in establishing its national sovereignty. Many important steps on the road to achieving national unity had been taken. However, there was much still to be done towards binding the different parts of the nation together and building up the national pride of Canadians.

The baby born to Fred and Norah Fisher on November 29, 1912, was to play an important and positive part in shaping Canadians' views about the country they lived in. John Fisher devoted many years of his life to praising Canada and arousing Canadians' enthusiasm for their country. His patriotic spirit and activities would eventually earn him the affectionate label "Mr. Canada" and the job of organizing the

The four-year-old future "Mr. Canada" enjoys the rural pleasure of a haystack, at home in Frosty Hollow, New Brunswick.

Centennial Year festivities to celebrate completion of Canada's first one hundred years of nationhood.

In 1912, of course, Canada's centennial was fifty-five years in the future and the nation was very different from what it is today. It was, for one thing, still struggling to emerge from the shadow of two powerful nations – its former ruler, Great Britain, and its nearest neighbour, the United States of America.

Only forty-five years earlier, Canada had been a colony ruled by Britain. In 1912, Great Britain was the centre of the British Empire, which included the huge land mass of India and many parts of Africa, and which was sometimes called "the empire on which the sun never sets". Britain's power – and its influence on Canadian politics and society – remained very great up until the end of World War Two.

In 1912, the majority of Canadians still had British roots. It was to Britain that many looked for leadership in foreign affairs, literature, ideas, and even Canada's national drink, which, at the time, was tea. Canadians read mostly British books. In school they learned more about Admiral Nelson and Trafalgar or Lord Wellington and the Battle of Waterloo than about Louis Riel and the Rebellion of 1885.

Canada's neighbour to the south was also a distractingly strong influence. The American nation was almost a hundred years older than Canada. Its population was ten times as large. The United States was big and powerful and rich – a world political, economic, and military force. American trade was important to Canada's economic well-being. American news was widely reported in Canadian newspapers. During John Fisher's young years, after radio came on the scene, Canadian airwaves were at first dominated by American programs and ideas.

It had been difficult for Canada to win its political independence from Britain. It had also been difficult to become a unified country reaching from sea to sea in the face of pressure – sometimes very strong pressure – to join the United States to the south. Maintaining the country's nationhood was an achievement Canadians could be proud of. Even so, in 1912 the nation was young and the ties binding it together were relatively few and weak.

In 1912, Canada's first prime minister, Sir John A. Macdonald, had been dead for only twenty-one years. The total population was just over seven million people, most of them living in rural areas and spread out in a thin line from east to west, close to the Canadian-American border. The different parts of the country still had little contact with one another. The Canadian Pacific Railway – the crucial coast-to-coast link for the scattered population – had been finished only twenty-seven years before, in 1885. There was no national newspaper. Wireless transmission of Morse code was in its infancy, and radio transmission of the human voice was in the experimental stage. (It was not until 1919 that the world's first commercial station, xwa in Montreal, later called cfcf, went on the air.) Automobiles were still a novelty in 1912, as were paved roads to drive them on.

The Canada of 1912 was a collection of loosely linked groups of people living on farms or in villages, small towns, and a few cities. The average Canadian in those days did little travelling. A trip of fifty or a hundred miles was a long one. Most people knew almost everything there was to know about their next-door neighbours, quite a bit less about the next town, and very little about their province or the country as a whole.

The establishment of a nationwide communications network was an important step in drawing Canadians closer together. The growth of radio in Canada helped give Canadians a better knowledge of their country as a whole, and played a major part in strengthening Canadian unity. A national radio broadcasting commission was established in 1932. In 1936 the Canadian Broadcasting Corporation (cbc) came into being with a network of radio stations to supply Canadian programs from one end of the country to the other.

A new medium of communication between far-flung parts of the nation was in place. The broadcasters who were to provide its content soon followed. Among them was a young man – John Fisher – whose enthusiasm for his native land was boundless. Fisher not only loved Canada, he had the great gift of helping other Canadians see why they should love Canada, too. Through the medium of radio, he soon set his feet on the road

towards becoming "Mr. Canada" – almost a national
symbol in his own right.

John Fisher's voice came over the national airwaves
for the first time during the darkest days of World War
Two, in the early 1940s. He talked about Canadians,
and he told them what a wonderful country they lived
in. He talked of the waving fields of wheat on the
Canadian Prairies, of the majestic Rocky Mountains, of
the emerging wealth of the northland and, above all, of
the superior qualities of Canada's varied peoples. He
called his programs "John Fisher Reports", and report he
did – from all across Canada. He waved the flag. He
wanted all Canadians to know he was proud to wave it
and he helped make them proud to wave it, too.

The Fishers of Frosty Hollow

Chapter 1

John Fisher's parents, Frederick Arnold Fisher and Norah
Wiggins, were both descendants of United Empire
Loyalist families who had fought on the losing side in
the American Revolution. These Loyalists chose to
emigrate to Canada when the war was over. Both the
Fisher and the Wiggins families came from the eastern
United States to the St. John River valley of New
Brunswick in the year 1783. The Wigginses were from
New Jersey and the Fishers were from New York State.

Both families had been fairly well off in the Thirteen
Colonies. But both families were also fiercely British in
their sympathies, and life outside the British Empire was
totally unacceptable to them. When the Thirteen
Colonies became the United States of America in 1783,
they cut their ties, took what they could with them, and
set out for the unknown bushland of Canada.

Their first winter was spent in tents covered with

*John Fisher's interest in travel
began at an early age. Here,
at age five, he gets behind the
wheel of the family car.*

birch boughs to help keep out the snow and cold. Because of the cold and hunger, many of the new immigrants didn't survive that winter. Those who did formed the backbone of a group that has always resisted the tide of U.S. influence. The Loyalists had already turned their backs on the United States, and they determined that their new land would remain true to the tradition of British ideals. One of John Fisher's great uncles, Charles Fisher, helped chart Canada's future course at the 1864 Charlottetown Conference that led to Confederation in 1867. He was almost one of the Fathers of Confederation, one of the people who gave Canada its first birthday party. So it was rather fitting that Charles's great nephew should be Centennial Commissioner, the man who planned Canada's hundredth birthday party.

John Fisher was born in Frosty Hollow, New Brunswick. Frosty Hollow today is part of the town of Sackville, New Brunswick. But when John Fisher was growing up it was a little country place, a community mostly of farm families. Some of the better-off townspeople had chosen to build their homes there, because it was close to Sackville. There were hills and streams, woodlots and grassy meadows where children could play and live out their childhood fantasies.

Just a few miles away was the town centre, with its brightly lit stores and Mount Allison University, where the children of the more prosperous families would proceed just as naturally as other children pass from grade to grade. There was no question of whether young John Fisher and his brothers and sisters would attend university, because money was never a problem for the Fisher family.

The main industry in Sackville was the Enterprise Foundry, which was owned and operated by the Fishers. The Enterprise kitchen stoves gleaming with nickel trim were famous for quality and beauty. They could be found in homes from one end of Canada to the other. Young John loved to visit the foundry. He was fascinated by the skills of the men who could turn moulds of sand filled with molten metal into handsome kitchen ranges.

He liked to talk with the foundry men. As one of them remembers: "He had a tremendous curiosity about

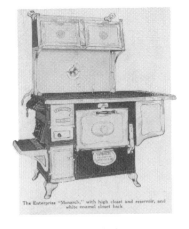

The Enterprise "Monarch," with high closet and reservoir, and white enamel closet back.

The Fisher family business was making Enterprise stoves, which were well-known across Canada. The Enterprise "Monarch" was a particular favourite.

how it was done, and about the different places we were shipping these stoves. He would stay around for hours, asking all kinds of questions. He wanted to know all about us and our families and where we came from. I asked him one time if he'd be coming into the business some day, and I remember being surprised when he replied: 'No, I don't think so.' "

There were five children in the Fisher family – three boys and two girls. John was set firmly in the middle.

According to John Fisher's brother George, as a young boy the future Mr. Canada was "scrawny, skinny, and shy". Mother Fisher joked that she was ashamed to take him out in public because he looked so underfed, but in fact he had the biggest appetite of anyone in the entire family. Young John was self-conscious about his skinny frame. It was his own idea to start a physical-fitness and weight-lifting program to develop his upper torso.

As a boy, John was strongly competitive in everything he did – in the games the family played at home, and in the competitions at Frosty Hollow's one-room school. After elementary school, he went to Rothesay Collegiate in St. John. He was always an average student, and a well-rounded one – involved in everything that was going on, from baseball and hockey to drama and debating. He wanted to do it all.

As his brother George recalled, John's biggest battle was with his shyness. It seemed to George that he was forever forcing himself into situations where he would have to talk and face up to people and situations. Members of the community often commented on the creativity and imagination of the young Fisher boy, who had a way with words in the debates at school. They didn't realize that these public appearances were a self-imposed torture he took part in to overcome his natural quietness.

John may have been trying to be like his mother's father. Dr. Cecil Wiggins was an Anglican clergyman who had preached the gospel in Sackville for forty-nine years and who lived with the Fisher family after he retired. The young Fishers had great respect for him. Dr. Wiggins read constantly and widely and encouraged his grandchildren to engage in daily discussions of current events.

After his retirement from the Anglican ministry, Grandpa Wiggins lived with the Fishers at Frosty Hollow. Another of John Fisher's ancestors had been an Anglican bishop.

Friends, family, and neighbours gathered on Sunday afternoons at the Fisher home in Frosty Hollow. John's father, Fred, is seventh from the right.

Family members still say that the "Mr. Canada" style of speaking was remarkably similar to that of Grandfather Wiggins. The old gentleman is remembered by the family as an effective and forceful speaker, sometimes a bit too forceful. The story is told of how he once reduced the pulpit to kindling wood while driving his points home. (There's no record that John ever pounded the furniture to bits, however.)

At the Frosty Hollow farm, "the latch was always open", especially on Sunday afternoons. George recalls that there was a constant parade of people from all walks of life. Most dropped by for lively discussions on a wide range of subjects. There were three topics that were constantly discussed: politics, religion, and making a living. John recalled that religion and making a living often took a back seat to politics and its effect on the growing nation. The shaping of the future "Mr. Canada" started early.

The Fisher children were always encouraged to take part in these verbal exchanges. Or they could simply sit and listen if they chose. John used these occasions to overcome his shyness.

He had further opportunities for this at Frosty Hollow Inn over near Boomer's Pond on the other side of town. Frosty Hollow Inn was listed at the time as one of the ten finest dining establishments in all of Canada. American visitors on their way to summer homes in the Maritimes would arrange to have at least a one night stay at the inn, an old converted house, where the specialties were seafood and hospitality. John liked to hobnob with the staff, who were mostly university girls working during the summer holiday season.

When John was almost ready for university himself, he took the important step of becoming bilingual. The

John Fisher, at seventeen, contemplates the future. This picture was taken in 1929, the year of the stock market crash and the beginning of the Great Depression.

Canadian Prime Minister at that time – about 1930 – was R.B. Bennett. The Prime Minister's brother, Ronald, lived in Sackville, and his family had boys of about the same ages as John Fisher and his brothers. When Prime Minister Bennett came to town in his private railway car the young Fishers and Bennetts thought it a great thrill to pay a call on him. Bennett welcomed them always, and told them stories about the glories of Canada.

During one of these visits, the Prime Minister pointed his finger at John and said: "Young man, if you want to get anywhere in this country, learn both languages." Fisher looked at Bennett, who was waiting for a comment, and replied unhesitatingly: "Yes, sir, I'll do that, I will."

The Prime Minister had hardly left town before Fisher made arrangements to enrol in a summer school at Trois Pistoles in the Province of Quebec. When he arrived there, however, he found that the lectures were far too advanced for him, so he slipped away and did what became his trademark for the rest of his life. He talked with the people in the streets of the town, trying to learn French that way.

He learned well. In fact, he learned so well that at the summer school's farewell dinner he was chosen to deliver the speech in French. His school instructors beamed with pride. Encouraged by his success, on the way home John delivered another speech to a trainload of cheering Québécois on a Gaspé railway platform. The experience apparently appealed to John, because he returned every summer for several years afterwards to live with Francophone families.

Young John fell in love with the French language and with French Canadian people, a love affair that was to last all his days. In those early Depression years, his new-found bilingualism combined with his father's own belief that travel was the greatest form of education were forming the embryo of super patriotism that was to earn him the title of "Mr. Canada."

Choosing a Direction — Chapter 2

The Fishers were socially prominent and wealthy, but the children weren't aware of those facts during their growing-up years. Their parents, Fred and Norah, brought them up strictly in the Anglican faith, and taught them the virtues of honesty and thrift, while expounding on the values of higher education.

In later years, John often remarked:

I never knew we had more than anyone else. Our clothes were no better than those of other children. We never had more money to spend than they did. We had a car, but so did a lot of others at that time. Our friends were just anybody we happened to take a liking to at school. My best friend all through grade school was the son of a man who worked as a labourer in my father's foundry, but I never knew what his father did for a living until years later. The subject never came up.

John Fisher's high school graduating class at Rothesay Collegiate, St. John, New Brunswick, in 1931. Fisher is fourth from the right in the front row. Classmate L. deB. Holly (second from right in the back row) also was to become a radio broadcaster. In later years, Fisher was a governor of Rothesay Collegiate.

It was not until he graduated from Rothesay Collegiate in 1931 that John realized the Fishers were a luckier family than most. By that time the full effects of the Depression were being felt, but it didn't seem to affect the Fisher family much. Sometimes John would hear his father saying how bad business was; that was all.

Honorary degrees were conferred on "Mr. Canada" by many Canadian universities, but the honorary doctorate from his alma mater, Mount Allison University, was his favourite.

That autumn, however, when John was enrolled in an Arts course at Mount Allison University, a lot of his high school friends who had planned to attend university didn't show up. The reason, of course, was lack of money. Their families had been hard hit by the Depression, and there was hardly enough money for food and shelter.

This bothered John a great deal, and embarrassed him too. He had not realized before that the Fishers were better off than other families in town. He wanted to quit many times. Each time, however, his parents convinced him that that would be foolish – that it wouldn't help anyone else anyway. So he kept on with his studies. John graduated with an Arts degree in 1934.

The Depression was showing no signs of weakening that year. John had had no idea of what he wanted to do with his life all through high school and university. Now he realized that the time for a decision was at hand. He could easily have joined the family business, but that seemed too simple a solution. Many of his friends and acquaintances had gone "riding the rails" to western Canada in search of work on farms. To the twenty-three-year-old John Fisher this seemed an attractive and adventurous thing to do. Besides, he was tired of books.

Here his parents stepped in to calm his enthusiasm, and again urged him to continue his studies. Perhaps it was because of a distinguished ancestor who had been Chief Justice of the Supreme Court that John finally decided to enter Dalhousie Law School in Halifax in the fall of 1934. Half-heartedly, he became a student once again. "I couldn't overcome the guilt I felt about living such an easy life while so many of my compatriots were literally existing from hand to mouth," he used to say later.

One of his fellow students was a tall, gangling young man from a Nova Scotia family that was also in the manufacturing business. This family business was underwear, not stoves, and the Stanfield name was

Robert Stanfield, a classmate during Fisher's student days at Dalhousie Law School, eventually became Premier of Nova Scotia, then leader of the Progressive Conservative Party.

"Scrawny and skinny" was the way Fisher was described as a young boy. He took up weight-lifting and body-building as a remedy. While at Dalhousie he became a member of the university wrestling team. Here he is shown shortly after winning the Maritime Intercollegiate Wrestling Championship for the third time.

famous all over North America. John's classmate was Robert Stanfield, who was destined to become Premier of Nova Scotia and, later, national leader of the Progressive Conservative Party of Canada.

Bob Stanfield and John Fisher often discussed the embarrassment they felt at belonging to families that could still afford to educate their children while half the country was lining up at soup kitchens. The influence of these feelings can be seen in the later lives of both men. John Fisher's speeches and writings glorified the accomplishments of the common man. Robert Stanfield became a crusading politician who introduced many social programs aimed at helping the poor of Nova Scotia. As Stanfield said: "The seeds of John Fisher's nationalism were born during his years at Dalhousie. He always spoke of Canada's potential and how he couldn't understand soup kitchens in a land that had so many riches."

At about this time, John's interest in weight-lifting and building up his body began to show some rewards. Gone was the "skinny, scrawny" look; John had become a handsome, muscular young man. He took an interest in amateur wrestling and had some success at the sport, becoming Maritime Intercollegiate Wrestling Champion three years in succession.

By now, too, John was discovering a talent for writing. Some of his items were published locally and in the university newspaper. At about this time he became acquainted with Hugh Mills, a local actor, who was having great success on CHNS, the only radio station in Halifax in the early Thirties. Hugh Mills had created a character for himself called "Uncle Mel". He did children's programs that consisted of music, stories, amateur contests, and dramas. The various roles were usually played by local children, but occasionally one of these plays required someone to play an adult role. When Mills approached Fisher about taking part, John hesitated at first. He thought he would be much too embarrassed, especially if his friends ever found out.

Uncle Mel persisted and finally convinced John that if he changed his voice "just a little", his friends would never know.

"That was how Mr. Canada got started," maintains Hugh Mills, who is now in his eighties. "It was then that

The Dalhousie Intercollegiate Wrestling Team in 1936. Fisher is on the far right.

he discovered not only the power of his own voice, but the power also of the still-young medium of radio. He was amazed to find letters coming in from all over Canada and much of the world in response to the drama productions."

In those days, the airwaves were not crowded with broadcasts from many different stations. As a result, with the right atmospheric conditions, even quite a low-powered transmitter could sometimes carry a program from Halifax to all corners of the earth. Listeners wrote in from Australia, from the British Isles, and from all parts of Europe to say that they had heard and enjoyed a particular broadcast.

By now John was also writing and broadcasting his own talks for CHNS. The law student who had joined a radio drama group as a lark was beginning to wonder if the Law really was the right career for him.

Chapter 3 A National Network for Canada

In 1936, something happened in Canada that would soon help John Fisher make up his mind about his future career. The CBC – the Canadian Broadcasting Corporation – was created.

Radio was the perfect instrument for binding a country as big and widespread as Canada together. Radio waves could reach into the farthest corners of the country – into prairie homesteads; into mountain villages; into the frozen wastelands of the north. It could solve the problems of Canadians' lack of communication with each other.

It could, but for a long time it did not. For years after the invention of radio, broadcasts were local not national. Small stations all across the country spot-lighted local talent, played records, and provided a news service of sorts. The news was mostly "scalped" – in other words, stolen from local newspapers. One station didn't know what the station a few miles away was doing, and there were no attempts made to connect all of these stations together into a smooth network.

At times, distant local stations could be heard, but that would only come about because of freakish atmospheric conditions that made for perfect reception. Most Canadian stations of the time were low-powered. Their normal listening range didn't usually go much beyond twenty-five to fifty miles. On the other hand, signals from powerful American stations had no trouble reaching into Canada, especially during the night hours when reception conditions were at their peak. These powerful stations sent out so strong a signal that they could block out the signals of Canadian stations completely.

Canadians could listen to their own stations with local content during the day. But at night they tuned in to massive doses of American culture. "Amos 'n' Andy", an early American comedy show, was followed with avid interest nightly by Canadians who couldn't name the current prime minister. This foreign domination of Canada's air waves worried many Canadians.

Gradually pressure was put on the government in Ottawa for some sort of system of national radio. The government-owned Canadian National Railway (CNR) was the first to respond. In 1923, it hooked up stations in Ottawa and Montreal for the first network program. Sir Henry Thornton, head of the CNR, thought radio would help keep passengers amused while they were travelling on trains.

Sir Henry was right. Passengers loved it, and before long there was a CNR network of stations all across the country, putting on high-quality music, talk, and news programs. The passengers were ecstatic, and so were the other Canadians who tuned in to these early broadcasts. It was Canada's first network. Although it was on the air only a couple of hours a day, it gave Canadians a taste for Canadian programming.

Then, on the first day of July 1927, an event took place that astounded the nation and turned the pressure for a national broadcasting system into a torrent of demand. The occasion was Canada's Diamond Jubilee celebration – Canada's sixtieth birthday. Coast-to-coast radio links had been hooked up for the occasion and, for the first time in the country's history, the words spoken by the Prime Minister and the sound of the chimes and bells on Parliament Hill were carried instantaneously to all parts of the country.

On that day, Canada took a giant step towards becoming a more united country. People saw that the nation's problems of great distance could be overcome by modern communications technology. Prime Minister Mackenzie King, in a speech he gave later, commented on the importance of what had happened:

On the morning, afternoon and evening of July 1, all Canada became, for the time being, a single assemblage, swayed by a common emotion, within the sound of a single voice.

As a direct result of that broadcast, Mackenzie King appointed a royal commission, with John Aird as

John Fisher and the Canadian Broadcasting Corporation both made a significant contribution to Canadian unity.

chairman, to study how best to establish a national radio network in Canada. The other commissioners were Charles Bowman, Donald Manson, and Augustin Frigon.

The Aird Commission's recommendations led to the founding, in 1932, of the Canadian Radio Broadcasting Commission (CRBC), under Chairman Hector Charlesworth. Public radio was launched in Canada. The CRBC set up a network of stations across the country. It did much of the pioneering work that eventually produced Canada's present system of national broadcasting.

Unfortunately, the funds provided for the new network were scanty. It limped along for four years, until 1936, when the CRBC was dissolved and the Canadian Broadcasting Corporation (CBC) was created to take its place. The CBC's task was to bring radio within the reach of all Canadians. More money was made available and more stations began to be built. New staff members were hired from different parts of the country. Many areas had been served only by private stations that carried few national programs. Now that too began to change.

Within months of its formation in 1936, the CBC quickly got off to a wonderful start with a low-budget program of music and good cheer called "The Happy Gang". Bert Pearl was the master of ceremonies, singer, and piano player. He was accompanied by a group of five or six musicians. The program opened with a "knock-knock" sound, followed by a voice calling: "Who's there?" Another voice would answer: "It's the Happy Gang!" "Well, come on in," the first voice would say heartily.

Canadians loved it! Here was a good program that they could call their own. Before 1936 passed into the history books, Bert Pearl and the Happy Gang were national celebrities, and people from coast to coast were knocking and yelling "Who's there?" The program remained on the air through the rest of the Depression, all through World War Two, and right up to 1959.

People working for local radio stations across the country were watching the fledgling network with keen interest. One of these was Harry Boyle. Boyle, who eventually became a senior executive of the CBC and later Chairman of the Canadian Radio and Television Commission, was then working at a small rural radio

CBC *Television was established in 1952. John Fisher was one of the first performers in the new medium.*

station in Wingham, Ontario. He remembers the effect the CBC had on many people in its early days:

> There were drama groups and things of that nature from the Atlantic to the Pacific, all doing their own thing. But there was no way for them to hear what others were doing until public broadcasting came along. There were bright young people in small communities starving for good drama and good music and it wasn't until the CBC came along that they satisfied their thirst. The CBC tied the country together and became a mecca for anyone who wanted to write or create.

From all over the country they came. Actors like John Drainie and Tommy Tweed. Writers like Len Peterson and Joseph Schull. Drama producers like Andrew Allan and Esse W. Llungh. They were full of excitement, enthusiasm, and idealism. They ached to spread their talents across the broader Canadian canvas offered by the CBC.

On the east coast, one of the first free-lancers hired was a young man still studying at Dalhousie Law School who was establishing a reputation as a storyteller on CHNS, the local Halifax station. His name was John Fisher. In Halifax, one of John's fellow actors in Hugh Mills's drama group had just been appointed Maritime regional representative for the new CBC network. His name was J. Frank Willis, and his job was to create a CBC presence in the Maritimes. There was no CBC radio station in Halifax, so Willis provided content for the new network, but used the studios of CHNS. He also asked free-lance artists and commentators that he knew he could depend on to provide material. John Fisher's pride-building talks, which had begun on CHNS, became part of the new programming on a CBC network of Maritime radio stations.

The Emerging Broadcaster

In the spring of 1937, John Fisher heaved a sigh of relief when he graduated from Dalhousie Law School. He tucked his degree away in a drawer for possible future use, and continued his work boosting the Maritime ego through his broadcasts on the new CBC, and in a column called "The Listening Post", in the Halifax *Herald*.

John had long been disturbed by what he often referred to as "that strangest of Canadian maladies; apology and non-support for all things Canadian". He

Twenty-four-year-old John Fisher, at home in Frosty Hollow in 1936. This was the year the CBC was formed. Although still studying law at Dalhousie University, Fisher had already gained some radio experience at CHNS in Halifax.

could see it first-hand in his own province, where people thought they weren't in the same league as their friends to the south. The author remembers Fisher expanding this point in one of many conversations over the years.

When I was growing up, the dream of most Maritimers was to emigrate to what was called "the Boston States". They were blind to the riches they had at home, and that was understandable. The newspapers and the radio were filled with stories of the glories of "the American way of life". These stories came in on the wires of American-based news services, and they were beamed in on the air waves. We were inundated with Americana – but there was practically nothing positive being written or broadcast about Canada. I resolved to change that.

John Fisher's resolve was translated into action long before he finished law school. His stories in the Maritime press and on CHNS, Halifax, were often lavish in their praise of individuals and points of interest that many people had previously taken for granted. For example, Fisher spoke of coal miners, who had never thought of themselves as anything but an oppressed minority slaving at tasks that nobody else would do, as "suppliers to industry; heaters of homes, and a group that made it possible for the rest of us to survive in a climate such as Canada's".

In a broadcast typical of that early Fisher period he said:

Outside of fishing I think coal mining is probably our oldest industry. French sailors were harvesting coal on the Atlantic side of Cape Breton as early as 1720. They tunnelled into the coal seams along the coast. They needed the coal to supply the great fortress of Louisbourg, down the coast just a few miles. The French built this massive fortress to defend their possessions in New France. They took twenty years to build it. The British captured it in 1758 and in 1760 destroyed it.

For many years Louisbourg had been little more than a small Cape Breton fishing village a few miles from Sydney. Until its restoration, the site yielded very few signs that a great fortress town had once existed there. However, visitors who examined it could see the outlines of the buildings and walls of the fort, long overgrown with weeds and grass. Cape Bretoners sometimes took their American relatives out to see these remains of the early days of European settlement in North America.

When Fisher's broadcasts got onto the national network, he often returned to the Louisbourg theme. The forgotten fortress made a good story, and Fisher liked to talk about interesting but neglected historical

monuments. However, in the late Fifties and early
Sixties, the federal government decided that restoring the
fort would make a good project for out-of-work coal
miners. The miners were retrained in the skills of the
eighteenth-century artisans who had originally built
Louisbourg. When the restored fort had become a
national historical site, famous all over the world, John
Fisher was still talking about it, this time, with glowing
enthusiasm, as "the largest reconstruction project in the
world".

In other stories and broadcasts, John Fisher told of
the proud Scots, banished by greedy landowners from
their native land, who had come to build a new society
in Nova Scotia. They had done it with nothing but
determination and backbone. He told of how their
ancestors had carved out homes from the unfamiliar and
frightening forests that covered the land. He praised
them for keeping their music, their Gaelic language, and
their culture alive.

He talked of Saint John, New Brunswick, as Canada's
oldest and proudest city, and of Prince Edward Island as
"the cradle of Confederation". A new pride came to the
Maritimes through the oratorical and writing skills of
one of its native sons.

There was no high-flying rhetoric in his style of
speaking. His message was simple and delivered in
straightforward language that anyone could understand.

When Fisher began to broadcast nationally, he refused to talk about a place he hadn't seen, so his job took him all over the country. He broadcast his talks "live" from local radio stations. Here he is shown in the studios of CKRC in Winnipeg.

All I did was eavesdrop on those who had a stake in their community
and told their story the way they would like to have it told.

For example, dulse is an edible seaweed very popular in
Passamaquoddy country. Drivers often keep it in the glove
compartments of their cars and reach in for a chew. Maritime kids in
theatres will dig into a bag of dulse. To landlubbers it has a horrible
taste, but to those born by the tides it's tasty and nutritious. And
loaded with iodine and vitamin c. I wonder how the history of Canada
might have changed had Champlain thought about the dulse along the
shore. He might never have gone across the bay to Port Royal in Nova
Scotia.

This was the kind of thing John Fisher did with such
great skill. He praised a Maritimer's passion for seaweed,
and sneaked in an "educational" historical reference to
Champlain and Port Royal along the way.

"My talks weren't meant to be objective," John said
once. "They were meant to be favourable. They were
'pride builders'."

This was an important period for John Fisher. The rest of his life was shaped by the talents he discovered in himself during the Thirties. Through his Maritime broadcasts and his writing for "The Listening Post" he was developing a very personal style. He was becoming known in the region as someone who could point out ways in which the Maritimes were more interesting than most Maritimers had ever dreamed.

John's taste for radio work soon began to outstrip his interest in the printed word. He was learning the techniques of broadcasting. From the letters that poured in from listeners, he knew he had a good radio voice and personality. He also realized very quickly the great power and influence that this new form of communication could have on Canadians' lives.

Hugh Mills ("Uncle Mel") who talked Fisher into taking his first radio broadcasting job for CHNS was later chosen by Fisher to be a member of the Centennial Commission. Here Fisher as Centennial Commissioner is shown discussing the merits of a centennial project with Hugh Mills and another commissioner, Marion Torinell. Marion Torinell was the only woman on the fourteen-person board.

World War Two played an important part in bringing John Fisher's talents to the attention of a wider audience. Fisher was twenty-seven years old when war

began in 1939. His law degree was still unused, and he was working as a reporter on general work for the Halifax *Herald*, which was the major shareholder in CHNS radio station. This allowed him to work in both newspapers and radio.

Like all young men of the time, there was nothing Fisher wanted to do more than join the fight against Hitler. He attempted many times to enlist, but was always turned down for medical reasons. Doctors thought his lungs were not healthy enough for active service.

Around him the city throbbed with the business of war. Recruitment centres were on every street corner. Troop trains loaded with new recruits pulled into the railroad station daily. The city was a centre for military operations of all kinds. There were ships from most of the friendly nations of the world. There were foreign submarines, war ships, and, of course, Canada's own Navy. On the streets of Halifax it seemed surprising to

Halifax was a busy city during World War Two, as this Barrington Street scene shows. Note the number of servicemen waiting to cross the street under the Buckingham sign.

Twice-weekly convoys left Halifax for beleaguered Britain carrying men and supplies. In this picture, taken in the early 1940s, one such convoy forms up in Bedford Basin before embarkation.

see someone in civilian clothes.

Halifax had always been a Navy city. During wartime, its naval activities multiplied a hundredfold. Halifax was the unnamed "Eastern Canadian port" referred to in newspaper stories. There, convoys formed up for the treacherous voyage across the Atlantic to Britain. Fifty ships at a time would be assembled in Bedford Basin to begin the zig-zag trip across the ocean. They carried soldiers and supplies for the beleaguered mother country. Enemy submarines operated all along the convoys' route, even outside the harbour entrance. Many ships were sunk even before the convoys got away from Nova Scotia waters. The war was indeed close to Canada.

There was constant activity as supplies and troops

moved into the city by land, then out again almost immediately by sea on the twice-weekly convoys. There were Canadian sailors, soldiers, and airmen. As well, the sound of up to twenty-five different languages advertised the presence of service people from all over the world. There were sailors from the merchant navy, workers from everywhere in the country pouring into Halifax to take jobs in the wartime industries around the city, and camp-followers of all sorts.

After the fall of France, Halifax harbour was alive, too, with ships of the French Navy, and the streets were full of French sailors. At times the normal population was quadrupled. The city was bursting at the seams.

As a reporter, Fisher found himself covering all the stories that he wished he could be actively participating in. He was there on the docks as the troop ships loaded their cargoes of men bound for the battlefields. He envied the young men their uniforms of khaki, navy, and air-force blue. He wanted to be with them, instead of just writing or broadcasting about them.

Fisher was still in constant touch with his friend Hugh Mills, better known as "Uncle Mel", the genial host of children's programs on CHNS. It was Mills who had enticed Fisher into radio as an actor. Like everyone else, Mills was doing all he could to help the war effort. One day he called Fisher into his office to tell him of a project that he, Mills, was involved in. As a member of the Halifax Theatre Arts Guild, Mills had been asked to put on concert parties for the troops gathered in Halifax to await their orders. Mills asked Fisher if he'd be willing to help.

The job had become immense because of the great numbers of troops that arrived in the city every day. Mills recalls that sometimes as many as seven shows a day were done at more than sixty different locations all over the city. Mills asked John, who was fluently bilingual by this time, to take on the responsibility for shows for the French troops. Fisher jumped at the chance. For the remainder of the war, he acted as producer and Master of Ceremonies for hundreds of French-language shows, which he put on wherever he could find an empty hall. John was there at the door to greet the lonely servicemen in their own language, and to bring to them a touch of home with familiar entertainment. He recruited French-speaking singers and musicians from the Maritimes. As often as he could he would be at the docks to wish the departing troops well as they boarded their ships.

At about this time, too, he was transferred completely to CHNS from the newspaper, so that he could devote his talents to radio. He originated a dance music program, called "John Fisher's Ballroom", which featured recorded music interspersed with morale-building stories. Hugh Mills says that this is where Fisher developed the style that was to make him a national radio star. It also satisfied Fisher's craving to do something meaningful for the war effort.

It would be just a matter of time before John Fisher would move from mainly local broadcasting to urging all Canadians, through the medium of national radio, to be proud of their country.

Halifax was teeming with servicemen waiting for postings. John Fisher was involved in finding entertainment for them. Here sailors and soldiers are lined up for admittance to the Halifax Orpheus Theatre in 1941.

"John Fisher Reports" Chapter 5

With the war over, John Fisher was transferred from Halifax to CBC Toronto to begin the series of radio talks, "John Fisher Reports", that would bring him international fame and the unofficial title of "Mr. Canada". That title was to stay with him until the day he died. "John Fisher Reports", broadcast at first on Sunday nights and later on Tuesday and Thursday evenings, brought his voice into millions of homes from one end of the country to the other.

In these upbeat broadcasts he unashamedly wore his love for Canada on his sleeve. He talked about the unique virtues of little-known communities and about aspects of Canadian folklore that most people had never heard of before. His broadcasts were pure Maritimes transposed to a national basis – and the nation responded.

Thousands of letters addressed to John Fisher poured into the national offices of the CBC: letters of praise, letters of pride, and letters of invitation for this new phenomenon, a Canadian radio star. Communities all across the country begged for his presence. "Come, see, and talk about us," they pleaded.

In an era when travel wasn't as swift or easy as it is today, Fisher was always on the move. He used cars, buses, trains, boats, small planes, and even dog teams to get where he wanted to go. He visited the isolated Magdalen Islands on the Atlantic seaboard. He travelled to the equally remote Queen Charlotte Islands on the Pacific Coast. Only a bush plane could land in the Northwest Territories when John Fisher first went there.

"There's no other way I can talk about this country unless I see these places myself," he once said. When friends expressed concern about the effects of so much travel on his system, he was apt to answer: "You can't

In 1947, the Manitoba government invited Fisher to tour and broadcast from the province's remote northern regions. A plane was supplied for Fisher and researcher Margaret Vollmer. The RCMP inspector hitched a ride.

On the 1947 trip for the Manitoba government, Fisher and researcher Margaret Vollmer flew to Flin Flon in the bush plane. Then, to reach more remote places, they set out by dog team.

get it from books. You've got to talk to the people themselves. Only they can tell you why they choose to live in places like Whiskey Creek, or Jackass Mountain."

As his fame grew, so did the calls for his time and his talents. In 1949, in addition to "John Fisher Reports", he undertook another series of Sunday night broadcasts, this time on a commercial basis for a well-known appliance manufacturer. The program, "Westinghouse Presents", featured a short talk by John Fisher, as well as popular songs sung by a fourteen-voice choir, the Don Wright Chorus. Promotions for various of the company's products were also included. The program ran from October until May each year. The company offered copies of John Fisher's talks to listeners, free of charge. It got thousands of requests for copies each week.

When listeners complained that the "Westinghouse Presents" broadcast time of 10:30–11:00 p.m. was too late in the evening, the CBC obliged by shifting it, in its third season, to six o'clock in the evening. That time spot had been occupied by "John Fisher Reports", which was now simply moved to Tuesday and Thursday evenings, where it gained many more thousands of listeners.

In the early 1950s, in response to a call from the pulp-and-paper industry of northern Ontario, which was having trouble recruiting and keeping workers, Fisher embarked on a series of speaking tours that took him to schools, chambers of commerce, and industrial companies to build interest in Canada's forests. He also undertook another series of pride-building reports, "People's Paper", broadcast over a network of northern Ontario stations. In a typical talk, forest workers would hear something like this:

Canada is a land of trees. We own more acres of forest per capita than any other people on earth. Our whole economy is tuned to the song of the saw. . . . The lumberjack . . . is the man whose strong arms drive the axe against the tree, and it is the ring of steel which starts one of the most thrilling stories in the world. . . .

The lumberjack is the pathfinder, the first of the papermakers. These men who march into Canadian forests are recorders of civilization.

All of John Fisher's broadcasts were done in his own very personal style of storytelling. To capture the listener's attention he would begin with a hint of mystery, as in this talk, which he called "The Romance of Seed":

Seed is Canada's cornerstone. Seed is also the story of life. Let me explain. Just the other day a fellow came to see me at home in Toronto. He wondered where I got all those radio stories of mine. I told him, "I don't have to move out of this town to find a story." I went further and said it wasn't necessary to leave the livingroom to find a story, to find romance. Romance lurks everywhere, sometimes in the humblest places. . . .

I told him that this room of ours is like any livingroom across Canada. It reveals the romance of seed. . . .

Look around your livingroom for a minute. Look at the walls, the furniture, your clothes, and then think how much you owe to nature, how much of your room and clothes came from a little seed that took root in the soil.

That chair or desk: it's made of wood. Where did the wood come from but a seed which germinated in the ground?

This, of course, made the listener curious about what Fisher would say next. It provided a springboard for the real subject of the talk, which was one Canadian farmer's achievement, in 1842, in finding a variety of wheat that would ripen quickly in the short Canadian summer.

When the forest industry was having difficulty recruiting workers, Fisher's talks on the "glories of the woods" and the "romance of paper" helped change the image of forestry. Here, in 1950, he is paying a visit to a modern mill in Fort William (Thunder Bay) in northern Ontario.

While he told this story, Fisher's famous enthusiasm came to the fore.

It was magic wheat, known as Red Fife. From that little stalk, almost eaten by a cow, a continent started to grow. Railways were built, towns appeared on the plains and men and women from all over the world headed for the Canadian prairies. . . . Canada became the breadbasket of the world. The West put new life into the Canadian economic dream.

John Fisher had clear and definite ideas about what would stimulate national pride and promote national unity. He was a firm believer in enthusiasm – in emphasizing the positive. He also believed that Canadians needed to know much more about their own country. A deeper understanding of one another by Canadians – who might live thousands of kilometres apart – was only possible if everyone had a greater knowledge of Canadian history and geography and of Canadian society as a whole. One of his foremost aims was to help educate Canadians about their country.

When Fisher took "John Fisher Reports" to little-known parts of the country, his presence was deeply appreciated.

Fisher's views were becoming more widely shared in the years after World War Two. The country was experiencing tremendous growth, not only in its population, its industry, and its economy, but also in its historical and cultural awareness. The appointment of a Royal Commission, chaired by Vincent Massey, to study the state of national development in the arts, letters, and sciences was one sign of this heightened national consciousness. The commission's report, published in 1951, recognized the importance of promoting a distinctively Canadian culture.

Canadians' overwhelming response to John Fisher's pride-building radio talks was another sign of awakening national self-esteem. Canadians were ready for the special blend of interesting (and often little-known) facts, enthusiasm, and eloquence that became John Fisher's trademark.

Fisher's own wide-ranging interests allowed him to approach the subject of "Canada" from many different angles. Sometimes he would give a talk in which he tried to appeal to every part of the country at once. In this quick "tour" of Canada's ten provincial capitals as they appeared in 1951, he did just that:

Every grammar school kid knows that Victoria is lovely, flowery and soft, cultivated and cultured.

We know that the "E" in Edmonton is for energy – bursting – you can almost see her grow. She stands for vigour, oil and advance – north country, crossroads town.

Regina, somehow, in her man-made parks reflects the friendliness and spirit of Saskatchewan.

Winnipeg . . . a breezy town with a big city face and a small town heart. Winnipeg is the hefty one of the West.

And then over the Christmas Tree land we roll till we reach Toronto. . . . Toronto somehow expresses the wealth, the promise, the cleanliness, the order of settled, rich Southern Ontario.

Now we go to Quebec City. . . . She sits all alone on a throne of rock, with a carpet of water below – as crisp as a Christmas card, which is what she is. Quebec is a study of dignity and determination.

Fredericton, in New Brunswick, is the Forest City. She stands like a page out of a romantic novel beside the river St. John – shaded under her spreading elms – the river city.

Charlottetown, the little one, leads a life all her own. She provides the hearth for the home on the waves. . . . Charlottetown is cosy.

Old Halifax – the city which says "halt" to ships of the sea – the city with the halo of tradition.

And what about the "S" and the "J" for St. John's, Newfoundland, you say? Well, friends, of all the cities of North America, St. John's, Newfoundland, is the oldest and in my view the most gracious or genteel. . . . Western friendliness without the breeziness or backslapping. No city can surpass St. John's in hospitality.

Sometimes Fisher would roam far back in time to report on interesting events in the country's history. In one talk he spoke about Martin Frobisher's search for the North West Passage. Frobisher found what looked like gold on Baffin Island in 1572 and a "gold rush" to Frobisher Bay took place in 1573, long before the Cariboo or the Yukon gold rushes of the nineteenth century.

Why, we were in the gold rush business almost fifty years before the Mayflower landed in New England. We had a gold mining boom in Canada before any Frenchman decided to settle in Canada. We were intrigued by gold before the Hudson's Bay Company ever caught a beaver, or even thought of it. And the prospectors and promoters and investors were not Frenchmen, Indians or Eskimos. Our first sourdough was a seadog. His name was Martin Frobisher.

Fisher became a national personality with his radio series. Crowds gathered for autographs and handshakes wherever he went.

One of Fisher's favourite themes was a contemporary

one – the rapid growth that was apparent in every area of Canadian life. At a time when the population was increasing rapidly, Fisher noted with pleasure that Canada was now a home for people from a great variety of races and cultures.

When the Second World War was over and relatives in the old lands of Europe wanted to communicate with blood links in Canada, they frequently sent merely the names of the parties addressed to "The Dominion of Canada". Thanks to a unique church in Toronto, the postal officials had no trouble at all. They simply forwarded them to the Church of All Nations because this church also acts as a post office – a church which has one huge open door for all faiths and tongues.

The enormous post-war expansion in Canadian industry was another topic dear to Fisher's heart. His interest in the romance of Canadian industry gave Fisher opportunities to praise the people whose labour was making the country strong. He loved to socialize with lumberjacks, miners, steelworkers, fishermen, and farmers. "The most interesting people in the country," he called them. He saw them as the builders, and others as "the housekeepers of those buildings".

He also delighted in pointing out things that were simply unusual, as in his broadcast about Canada's "wackiest and smallest tourist attraction", the Magnetic Hill near Moncton, New Brunswick:

It all happens because of the tricks of Mother Nature in a capricious mood. It is an optical illusion. And you can look at it all day and still swear the hill goes up. But when your car starts rolling backwards, lickety-split, you know it must be going down.

Fisher could bring the same overflowing enthusiasm to the small as well as the immense because of his strong belief that Canada's best hope for unity lay in recognizing and celebrating the marvellous variety within its borders. He repeated this message over and over again, in different words and in many different places, saying: "I roam this country, probing, portraying, and prodding with but one purpose: to awake Canada to its true potential. Each corner of Canada stabs my soul, for I am in love with the whole."

To this self-appointed task of making Canadians more aware of their proud heritage he brought many talents. He had the right spirit. He had the magic of a voice that was not just compelling but was also filled with friendliness. It was what has been called a salt-water voice – a voice tinged with the flavour of "down home". With that great voice and his superb choice of words that just seemed to roll out, John conjured up pictures that no television screen has been able to match.

He had the uncanny ability to make you ache to live in the place he was talking about. One listener wrote to the CBC president at the time, A. Davidson Dunton, to say: "Last week he had me all set to move to the Okanagan Valley of B.C. as the best place in Canada. This week, because of his broadcast, I believe that the very best place is the Annapolis Valley of Nova Scotia." That's the way many Canadians were affected by the exuberance and love that John Fisher put into his broadcasts about Canada.

Canadians responded enthusiastically to this voice prodding it into patriotism over the air waves. John's first series of broadcasts drew 27 000 requests for script copies – something totally unheard of before. Letters poured in at the rate of 1500 a week.

As his broadcasts continued, his fame grew and communities all over the country clamoured for a personal visit from him. He accepted as many invitations as humanly possible – sometimes as many as seven in one week – and he travelled hundreds and thousands of kilometres, back and forth across the country. In his first five years on the national scene, he logged more than 210 000 kilometres.

During these visits, he was always invited to speak in public, something he did with great skill and gusto. He spoke in factories, hockey rinks, schools, and drill halls.

The Fisher family. John Fisher, his wife, Audrey Paynter, and their son, John, Jr., in 1951 at the height of Fisher's fame as a broadcaster. Mrs. Fisher died in 1966. Fisher remarried in 1974.

Fisher often took his family on holidays to the places he had visited on his workaday travels. Here, at Deception Pass, about sixteen kilometres northeast of Lake Louise, Fisher, his son, John, Jr., and his nephew, Peter Tapley, raise their eyes to Ptarmigan Mountain. Fossil Mountain is in the background.

Wherever he spoke, people jammed in to hear him.

His fame spread across the border to the United States and he became the Canadian most in demand as an after-dinner speaker. His topic was always the same – Canada. In the early Fifties, Fisher was receiving more than a thousand requests annually to appear as guest speaker at conventions and at service and study clubs in Canada and the United States. He couldn't possibly do that much, of course, but his close friend and colleague, Lou Cahill, reported that it wasn't for want of trying. He remembers one day in particular when John actually did make four separate speeches, beginning with a breakfast talk in one town, a luncheon speech in another eighty kilometres away, a talk with school children in the same town during the afternoon, followed by a wild car ride back to the town where he had started his day for an after-dinner speech that night.

These talks were inevitably followed by scores of people crowding around wanting to shake Fisher's hand or asking for his autograph. As Mr. Cahill recollects:

Fisher enjoyed seeing all parts of Canada first-hand and dressing to fit the part. In this 1949 photo he is prepared for a visit to the Northwest Territories.

John never gave anyone the impression that he was pressed for time. He enjoyed meeting people as much as they enjoyed meeting him – indeed, something that one of them said could easily show up in his next speech. I remember on that particular day I was so tired at the end I could hardly move, but John stayed up until the early hours of the morning, talking and listening to the stories of the local people. It's interesting to note, too, that each of his talks that day was different –

Like an electioneering politician, Fisher met and kissed his share of babies. Here, in 1950, he meets the Hargreaves quadruplets of Sault Ste. Marie.

In the days before regular air services made many places accessible by plane, Fisher did much of his travelling by train. Here Fisher and his friend Lou Cahill stroll the platform at White River, Ontario, in 1949.

each one delivered without notes, and each one as fresh as the one that had gone before. The next morning my phone rang at 6:30. It was John reminding me that we had to have an early breakfast as we were due at another town a hundred miles away for a luncheon speech.

John's brother George thinks the spark of Fisher's nationalism was kindled by the writings of the New Brunswick poet, Sir Charles G. D. Roberts, who was known as "The Bard of Tantramar." (The Tantramar is a river that winds its way through the marshy country of New Brunswick.) "Canadian am I in blood and bone," Roberts had written. Fisher often quoted this and another stirring line of the poet's: "Awake, my country, the hour is great with change."

John Fisher, Canadian "in blood and bone", took up the challenge of Charles G. D. Roberts. In his efforts to awaken his country, however, Fisher was not afraid to vary his methods from time to time. Not all of his broadcasts praised and exalted Canada and the achievements of Canadians. "I don't praise Canada as much as I prod it," he used to say. Sometimes he scolded Canadians into making an effort to preserve their heritage, as in this broadcast from the late 1940s:

We have been mean to our own Canadian youngsters. Through neglect we have robbed them of much of their birthright. We have stolen many of the historic sights which should thrill their eyes. Listen to a few of them! Where is Champlain's astrolabe or compass which was lost when he was the first white man to go West? They found it near Renfrew, Ontario, a few years ago. This priceless possession was sold to a tourist from New Jersey. The most valuable table in Canada, the Confederation Table from Quebec, was sent to the Northwest Territories as office furniture. . . . The original documents of the Charlottetown Conference are in a building which could go up in smoke in a matter of minutes. Our National Museum in Ottawa is so crowded that pictures of the First World War are locked in the basement.

We have no National Library, but Ethiopia has. Lower Fort Garry, outside Winnipeg, although well-kept, is a private golf and social club. Montgomery's Tavern in Toronto, where the Mackenzie Rebellion was hatched, was torn down to make room for a small fruit store and shoe repair shop. How many Canadians know that Uncle Tom of Uncle Tom's Cabin lived in Canada for thirty years and died here? How many Canadians have ever heard of Billie Green, the Canadian Paul Revere? This young boy, by a nocturnal walk through the bush, saved the Niagara Peninsula for the British.

Can you take any more? The great epic poem on the Acadians was written by Longfellow, an American. Or take the case of St. Lawrence Market, about two miles from my office in Toronto. The defenses of the War of 1812 were planned there. There, they set up the under-ground railway for escaping slaves. There is not even a plaque on the building.

Many of the things that, in 1949, Fisher said should be done were eventually done. Fisher's scolding helped start the ball rolling on many projects like these across the country. He kept on prodding Canadians whenever he felt they needed it.

He had many positive recommendations to accompany the harsh words, too. These came out almost like commands.

How can we be true or strong when we, through neglect, rob tomorrow's citizens of links with the past? . . . We in Canada should work harder at selling our own story. We should let imagination run. We should gather our treasures, put them on a freedom train and take them from one end of Canada to the other. We should set up more endowments and scholarships. . . . Certainly it will cost money, so does a bomber, so does a bridge.

When he wrote that passage, John Fisher did not yet know that in Centennial Year those very recommendations would be carried out – or that he was destined to play an important part in making them happen.

Chapter 6 Centennial in the Making

In 1956 Fisher left broadcasting to become Executive Director of the Canadian Tourist Association (CTA). The war was now more than a decade in the past and travel was easier for ordinary people to afford. Tourism was becoming big business. It was John Fisher's job to encourage more of those travel dollars to be spent in Canada by opening people's eyes to the natural delights that Canada had to offer. For years, Fisher had praised his country to his fellow Canadians and, on his speaking tours, to selected groups of Americans, too. His new CTA job gave him the chance to sell Canada to the world.

For the next five years, all over North and South America, in the British Isles, and in Europe, Fisher worked enthusiastically to attract new visitors to Canada. Within the country itself, his "See Canada First" campaign aimed to persuade Canadians to spend their vacation dollars at home.

Fisher was doing valuable work for the country in this job with the CTA. But it was not long before an opportunity arose for him to do something that he felt would be even more worthwhile. In 1961 he was invited to join Prime Minister John Diefenbaker's staff as the P.M.'s special assistant. The two men, Diefenbaker and Fisher, shared a number of important ideas and qualities. They both had great dreams for Canada and they both used unique speaking styles and colourful phrasing to captivate audiences. When Diefenbaker was travelling the country in the 1957 election campaign he spoke in his own dramatic style of Canada's unparalleled resources and of a north country that was crying out to be developed. He referred to it as his "Northern Vision". He called for "roads to resources", new highways that would open up previously unexplored parts of the country.

Prime Minister John Diefenbaker with his new special assistant, John Fisher, at the Military Institute in Toronto, in 1961. Fisher supplied little-known facts about little-known places and Diefenbaker provided the oratory.

The voters responded to Diefenbaker and, by June of 1957, for the first time in twenty-two years, Canada had a Progressive Conservative government. (Diefenbaker's Conservative predecessor, R. B. Bennett, had also had an influence on John Fisher's life.)

Diefenbaker's belief in the richness of Canada's regions produced a number of new programs. Highways to undeveloped areas were built. So were new railways. Exploration for Arctic oil and gas became more important. All of this formed the beginning of a national energy policy. That policy, in turn, led to the creation of the National Energy Board. First attempts were also made to compile an inventory of Canada's known natural resources.

All of these things delighted John Fisher, who had an abiding interest in all parts of Canada. Better still, he had the sort of "feel" for the whole country that Diefenbaker admired and valued. "Dief" was a westerner with prairie pioneer roots. He was very proud of his homesteader background. But he lacked detailed knowledge of much of the country.

Resplendent in his crown and robes, John Fisher appears as King of the Saranac Lake Winter Carnival in 1958. After his radio program "John Fisher Reports" ended in 1955, Fisher continued to be much in demand for guest appearances at such events across the country.

The Prime Minister had listened to and enjoyed John Fisher's broadcasts for years. In his radio talks, Fisher described nooks and crannies of Canada that the Prime Minister had never heard about before. Fisher was the perfect person to supply the interesting but little-known facts about out-of-the-way parts of the land that would make the Prime Minister sound like "a man for all of Canada". Local people and institutions, local issues, local popular opinion – John Fisher knew about them all.

Diefenbaker believed in fighting for the underdog. Fisher knew how to praise what was previously unrecognized. Now Fisher supplied the speeches and Diefenbaker delivered them in his dramatic style. Audiences all over the country, whether they lived in Joe Batt's Arm, Newfoundland, or Hundred Mile House, British Columbia, warmed to this "prairie boy" prime minister, who knew so much about them. By contributing the kind of stories he had been telling for years, Fisher helped to humanize the prairie lawyer occupant of the Prime Minister's Office.

This period also helped Fisher promote his own idea of having "the biggest birthday party ever held" for Canada's one hundredth anniversary of Confederation. Fisher had been talking about this since the early 1950s. During the thousands of kilometres he and Diefenbaker travelled together, Fisher couldn't help pushing the idea.

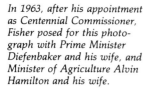

In 1963, after his appointment as Centennial Commissioner, Fisher posed for this photograph with Prime Minister Diefenbaker and his wife, and Minister of Agriculture Alvin Hamilton and his wife.

After their first meeting in Ottawa, in 1964, the directors of the Centennial Commission held meetings once a month in different provincial capitals. The fourteenth meeting was held in September 1965, in St. John's, Newfoundland. On that occasion, Chief Commissioner John Fisher presented Premier Joseph Smallwood with a desktop Centennial Flag.

His enthusiasm was catching. The country had caught it from his radio broadcasts. Now the Prime Minister caught it too.

Diefenbaker gave Fisher the green light to make his idea a reality when he appointed him Chief Centennial Commissioner in 1963. It was four years before the birthday party. Fisher immediately began laying his plans. To do the job he would need people who shared his love and enthusiasm for Canada. Through his travels he was already acquainted with hundreds of excellent candidates. Fourteen directors were chosen from across the country. One of them was Hugh Mills ("Uncle Mel"), Fisher's old friend from Halifax. Mills was Fisher's kind of man – the sort of Canadian who had an intimate knowledge of the region he lived in. The remaining directors, from the various regions of Canada, had similar qualifications. There were 110 other members with lesser degrees of responsibility. In total, then, 125 people, representing the broad mosaic of Canadian society, sat on the commission.

The first meeting of the full commission was held in early 1964 in the railway committee rooms in Ottawa. Fisher stood up and welcomed the members of his new commission. What followed was, according to Hugh Mills, the most amazing feat of memory he ever witnessed. Without notes or a script of any kind, John Fisher introduced each of the 125 members. "Not only did he introduce us," said Mills, "he had some little personal thing to say about every one of us."

At the end of the introductions, Fisher said simply, "Ladies and gentlemen, we have a big job ahead." After a moment of stunned silence at the Fisher performance, the group broke into an ovation that lasted for five minutes. "Then," says Mills, "we all went to work."

The commission was given a budget of $200 million. The money was to be distributed to worthy projects on a shared basis. When a group proposed a particular scheme – a new museum, for example – it would have to come up with one third of the money itself. A similar amount would come from the provincial government. The remaining one third would be granted by the commission. Over the next three years, the commission considered and approved thousands of applications.

For the most part, things went smoothly and according to plan. But there was conflict, too. Members would fight for pet projects. Different groups representing different areas of the country sometimes competed with each other. Liberal and Conservative members of the commission also found themselves on opposite sides.

In spite of the inevitable conflicts, the whole country agreed that when the big event took place, the commission had done a good job. Of the $200 million the commission set out to distribute, there was only $178 thousand left at the end of 1967.

According to Fred McGuinness, a commission member from Alberta, "the centennial celebration was a high point in this country's history. It was the right idea at the right time and it couldn't have been brought off without John Fisher, a man with unique gifts – a raconteur without equal and a superb crowd psychologist."

If Fisher had a weakness, it was in the area of administration, a field in which he had little previous experience. Like the Prime Minister who had appointed him, Fisher sometimes seemed unwilling to delegate authority to the members of his own staff. Because the project was so important to him personally, Fisher was flying all over the country to speak in support of his dream. On his return, he would be upset to find that decisions had been made in his absence. He viewed such occasions as attempts to interfere with his running of the

Wherever Fisher travelled in the years leading up to Centennial Year, he was the recipient of unusual gifts and mementoes.

Fisher travelled the country for three years building excitement prior to Centennial Year. He appeared on hundreds of radio and television programs (here "Front Page Challenge") as a guest.

Secretary of State Judy LaMarsh and Centennial Commissioner John Fisher present a jolly public presence in early 1965. Their behind-the-scenes battles for control of the centennial plans were referred to by staff as "The John and Judy Show".

commission. On the other hand, it seemed to many commission members that Fisher "wanted his finger in every pie."

Among these conflicts, the most serious were those between Fisher and Minister of State Judy LaMarsh, who had the Centennial Commission in her portfolio of cabinet responsibilities. To LaMarsh, the centennial represented fun, action, headlines, people. Often LaMarsh would want to push a pet project. Often she would take action without Fisher's knowledge or permission. Sometimes Fisher would not learn of her activities until he saw a newspaper article about something she had just announced. Fisher would react angrily. The battles between them at commission meetings were referred to by commission members as segments of "the John and Judy Show."

It was the feeling among some of the members that LaMarsh envied Fisher his role as Chief Commissioner and would gladly have given up her own cabinet position in exchange for Fisher's job. They also felt that she made his job more difficult. She was often critical of him, sometimes even in public.

Surprisingly enough, however, some commission members feel today that the tensions in the centennial office didn't hinder the over-all effort. More than that, they think the disagreements may have helped to produce a more lively program.

A look at Canada during Centennial Year gives an idea of just how lively and worthwhile that program proved to be.

Centennial Year Chapter 7

For Canada, the year 1967 was a successful and joyous occasion that went beyond the dreams of everyone. From coast to coast, Canadians threw themselves into the celebration of Canada's one hundredth birthday in crazy, wonderful, and meaningful ways to demonstrate pride in their country.

Canada's Centennial Year opened on New Year's Eve, December 31, 1966, with a message, delivered from Parliament Hill, from Her Majesty, Queen Elizabeth the Second:

As we begin our celebrations, I pray that God will continue to bless Canada as you move into your second century, confident of your own destiny and purpose.

A few seconds past midnight, January 1, 1967. The crowds on Parliament Hill, Ottawa, join with the dignitaries to sing "O Canada" to open the centennial celebrations. From left to right, Mrs. Roland Michener, Senator Maurice Lamontagne, Governor General Roland Michener, Secretary of State Judy LaMarsh, and Centennial Commissioner John Fisher.

Fisher with John Diefenbaker's successor, Liberal Prime Minister Lester Pearson.

Her Majesty was followed by Centennial Commissioner John Fisher, reading the special prayer:

Almighty God, who has called us out of many nations and set our feet on this broad land, establishing us as one people from sea to sea, gratefully we remember how Thou hast led us through one hundred years. Grant Thy blessing on the joyous celebration of our centennial year, and a deeper worthiness of the dreams that gave us birth, that with the flame of freedom in our souls, and the light of knowledge in our eyes, we may magnify Thy name among men, one country serving Thee.

At the conclusion of John Fisher's prayer, Prime Minister Lester Pearson stepped forward to light the Centennial Flame, which would burn throughout 1967, symbolizing the pride of all Canadians. "Tonight we let the world know," said the Prime Minister, "that this is Canada's year in history."

Pearson's words were prophetic. The country had never seen anything like Centennial Year. Canadians all tried to outdo each other in demonstrating their pride.

Almost every community had a centennial project. There were giant sports complexes, libraries, and art centres, to say nothing of hundreds of smaller projects. Small or large, every project instilled community and national pride.

Bowsman, Manitoba, completed a sewer centennial project to prove it was ready for Canada's second century. As a crowning touch, on New Year's Eve, 1966, the townspeople set a torch to a giant bonfire fuelled by all the outhouses in town. The story not only made news around the world; it also reached many a tiny Canadian hamlet with plans for its own special project. The year was off to a fun start.

Before the first day was over, from countries around the world, messages of congratulations and the sounds of bells from many foreign capitals were beamed into the CBC's national network. The excitement was contagious. As the New Year moved across the seven time zones of Canada, bells rang out in provincial capitals and tiny hamlets alike. The centennial flame had ignited centennial enthusiasm.

John Fisher had spent four years and travelled many thousands of miles to produce the enthusiasm he felt Canada's hundredth birthday party deserved. At first cynics had sniggered and derided his efforts, saying there was no way you could pull so few people together in so many acres of land. There was just no way to create community feeling in a country as cold and spread out as Canada. It shouldn't be a country, some said. It never was a country, others declared. John Fisher paid them no heed.

He set out in 1963 to prove them wrong, and he did what he knew best; he travelled and goaded and glorified. He opened local people's eyes to the assets they had always had.

In Sudbury, Ontario, he told them: "For Heaven's sake, don't you realize you're the world's leading producer of nickel? You're unique in the world." The collective chest of Sudbury swelled with pride. The city erected a huge reproduction of a five-cent piece – a nickel. The gesture appealed to people, and the Sudbury nickel still attracts the attention of visitors to northern Ontario.

Official portrait of Canada's Chief Centennial Commissioner, with the official logo in the background.

On the west coast, Fisher visited one fishing community that said plaintively that it had nothing to dress up. "Nothing?" said Fisher. "What about that old wharf down there? History is oozing out of its planks and pilings. Clean it up and turn it into a tourist attraction." The townspeople did. Many communities, at his urging, produced books of local history. Others put together regional cookbooks.

Everywhere he went, Fisher gently scolded the nation for its blindness. At a convention of hoteliers, he said it was time for them to put an end to their lethargy and let their hair down. "Doll up, spruce up, and put on some powder and paint." He visited countless Home and School Associations, and told them: "Canada has been lounging on the psychiatrist's couch so long that it doesn't know how to get up."

He told the citizens of many cities and towns to clean up their parking lots, which, according to him, looked "like bombsites". He scolded them about the highway approaches to town, which he called "treeless wastelands of garish signs". He pleaded, coaxed, and cajoled. Gradually, as he gave ideas and planted seeds of others, most cynicism changed to optimism, and, finally, enthusiasm.

By the time 1967 rolled around, almost every Canadian was involved in at least two centennial projects – one for his community and one for himself.

People built centennial houses and took centennial university courses. Thousands quit smoking as personal projects. Student groups went out with paint brushes to spruce up neglected buildings. They cleared up the littered beds of streams; they "adopted" lonely senior citizens. The spirit of John Fisher became truly the spirit of the nation. The opening ceremonies for Centennial Year were the signal for eighteen million Canadians to begin a year-long tribute of love to their country. They expressed it in many ways.

One group of mountains in the Rockies, near the Yukon-Alaska border was named Centennial Range, and the Alpine Club of Canada set out to climb every peak – one for the Centennial itself, and one each for the ten provinces and two territories. Fifty-two climbers, working in teams, planted territorial, provincial, Canadian, and centennial flags on all of them.

Great entertainment spectacles took off on cross-country tours. Les Feux Follets and the National Ballet performed in towns and cities across Canada that had never before seen live classical performances. *Anne of Green Gables*, the musical commissioned by the Charlottetown Festival and based on the books of Lucy Maud Montgomery, went travelling, too, from one end of Canada to the other. A special train pulled out of Halifax with Nova Scotia square dancers on board. They danced on every station platform between Nova Scotia and Vancouver. Each time the train pulled away from a station, the number of dancers on board had increased. By the time the train reached the west coast, the fifty original dancers had grown to three hundred and twenty-five.

The Canadian Armed Forces also travelled the country, presenting a panoramic spectacle of Canadian history, put on by 2500 performers. The RCMP Musical Ride criss-crossed the country, presenting its own well-loved spectacle to small-town audiences that had never before seen it "live". Hot on the heels of the horses and the red-coated Mounties was a show featuring thirty-one motorcycle riders. The Armed Forces Display Team thrilled audiences with its dare-devil performances and its precision timing.

A Toronto man trained his Mynah bird to sing "O Canada". Musical comedy star Carol Channing, in

Toronto with the musical *Hello, Dolly*, stopped her performance one evening to show that she, too, knew the words of "O Canada."

In Montreal an island had been built in the river as the setting for Expo '67. This has been called the greatest-ever world's fair. At Expo, exhibits from every province, both territories, many of Canada's cities, and a multitude of foreign nations made the fair an exciting spectacle and won it much praise. Expo '67, drew millions of people from all parts of the globe.

It drew their leaders too. The last remaining emperor in the world, Haile Selassie of Ethiopia, came, as did the President of the United States, Lyndon B. Johnson. The Queen, and the Prime Minister of Britain, Harold Wilson, also paid Canada the compliment of a visit. Prince Philip opened the Pan-American Games in Winnipeg and the Royal Winter Fair in Toronto.

Every foreign vessel that passed anywhere near Canadian waters made a special point of pulling in to a Canadian port to deliver greetings.

Sir John A. Macdonald, one of the Fathers of Confederation and Canada's first prime minister, would have been 152 years old in 1967. Since he couldn't attend the celebrations, the citizens of Kingston, where his remains are buried, threw him a party anyway on his birthday, January 11th. They built a huge, eight-tier birthday cake, and there was enough for everybody. John Fisher got frosting all over his face. However, there

Although Expo '67, sometimes called "the greatest world's fair ever", figured prominently in Centennial Year, it didn't come under the responsibility of the Centennial Commission. John Fisher, who was often there, got through the gates by showing his Press pass.

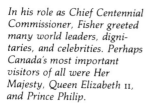
In his role as Chief Centennial
Commissioner, Fisher greeted
many world leaders, dignitaries, and celebrities. Perhaps
Canada's most important
visitors of all were Her
Majesty, Queen Elizabeth II,
and Prince Philip.

was nothing on John's face but a great big grin when he
dressed up in a top hat and late-eighteenth-century
clothing to celebrate the 1785 founding, by fur trader
Simon McTavish, of the Beaver Club in Montreal. Fisher
was also at the party for Robbie Burns thrown by
Canadian Scottish fans of the poet. On that occasion
Fisher assured the audience that haggis was one of his
favourite dishes.

Fisher was everywhere. He was in St. John's,
Newfoundland, when hundreds of ships and thousands
of people gathered to re-enact the arrival of the explorer
John Cabot on the shores of North America. And he
was present when Canada sent out an expedition to
attempt to find the grave of explorer Sir John Franklin,
who died in the Arctic in 1847.

John Fisher glowed with pride as one project after
another began, or was completed, across the land. Most
satisfying of all were the Centennial Train and the
tractor-trailer caravan that carried the story of Canada's
history across the continent. These were travelling
exhibits that traced Canada's history and development
from the tropical forests of a million or more years ago
all the way up to the latest technological miracles of
1967.

The exhibits had been years in the planning. Visitors
to both train and caravan felt like time travellers, so
realistic were the displays. The cave dwellers of
prehistoric times, the Fathers of Confederation, the
industrial marvels of the twentieth century, and many
other scenes and events, past and present, were vividly
shown.

John Fisher was there himself on many occasions. He would escort groups of school children or adults, and add his own voice to the recorded commentary.

The horn on the Centennial Train was specially altered so that it would sound the first four notes of "O Canada". The train stopped in large cities and in whistle stops, and more than two million visitors went through it. Hundreds of thousands of people also passed through the motorized caravan.

There was a Centennial Flotilla – a fleet of boats – with similar displays. It floated down the Mackenzie River, stopping at outposts along the way, bringing the exhibits to remote northern communities. The flotilla also carried entertainers and samples of exciting events that northerners might otherwise miss. John Fisher had thought of everything.

For something a little different, he organized the great Centennial Canoe Pageant. Canoeists in birchbark canoes re-lived the days of the *voyageurs*, taking part in

Fisher donned voyageur costume at the canoe pageant trials in 1966. The pageant itself, in 1967, took the form of a 104-day race from Rocky Mountain House, Alberta, to Expo '67 in Montreal.

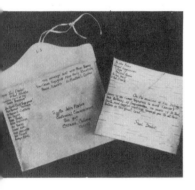

The winning canoe team in the 104-day canoe race carried a greeting on rawhide from Manitoba's Premier and the Provincial Secretary. A message on birch bark enclosed in a leather pouch was also part of the winning canoe's cargo. Fisher was there at the Expo '67 finish line to accept it.

a 104-day race from Rocky Mountain House, Alberta, to Expo '67 in Montreal. Seventy-two twentieth-century *voyageurs*, six in each of twelve canoes, representing all the provinces and territories, faced the same conditions as the original *voyageurs* had. Like their forerunners, they battled the white water of northern rivers – and they seemed to have fun doing it. The CBC carried daily reports of their progress on radio. When they landed at Expo in September, John Fisher was there to accept a message written on birchbark, which they had carried in a leather pouch all the way.

A group of Jesuit priests also staged a six-month canoe pageant in tribute to their brethren, the early missionaries, who had played such a large part in opening up the wilderness.

At the Centennial Trapper's Festival in The Pas, Manitoba, all the members of the Manitoba Legislature showed up waving Canadian and centennial flags. Trapper Joe LeClerc, who had been appointed special postmaster for the occasion, took his mailbag and set out to "mush" his dog team the 960 kilometres to Prince Albert, following the exact course of the old mail route.

Farther north, in the Northwest Territories, a Centennial Sourdough Festival was held. Sourdough was a fermented bread dough popular with prospectors during the days of the Klondike Gold Rush. Early prospectors borrowed the word and referred to themselves as sourdoughs. At the Sourdough Festival – a feast of eating, music, and dancing – everyone was an honorary sourdough and dressed to fit the part. Although the festival still takes place today, most people agree that the fervour with which it was first celebrated in 1967 has yet to be equalled.

Inventing new celebrations became a national pastime. The City of Edmonton borrowed from two cultures to stage a Centennial Mukluk Mardi Gras. The French Mardi Gras (literally translated as "fat Tuesday"), which is celebrated on Shrove Tuesday, is a traditional day of feasting and celebrating immediately preceding the strict fasting laws of Lent. Mukluks are the high skin boots worn by Native People of the far north. During the Edmonton celebrations the streets were alive with all nationalities as they joined hands, eating, drinking, and feasting, their feet snugly immersed in mukluks.

For the first time, in honour of Canada's birthday, the Lunenburg, Nova Scotia, County Fair Exhibition was an international event. In the annual ox-pulling contest at Bridgewater, Nova Scotia, the Canadian team, with much grunting and groaning, beat the American team to take the top three prizes. Nothing was impossible for Canadians that year.

To prove the truth of that, eighty-four-year-old Howard Silver scythed his way to the top prize in a centennial hay-cutting competition, and a 109-year-old woman demonstrated her pride by singing "How Great Thou Art" on national radio.

Composer Bobby Gimby wrote a love song for the Centennial. He called it "Canada (We Love Thee)". Thousands of enthusiastic Canadians wrote letters to newspapers and phoned radio stations demanding that it be adopted as the country's new national anthem.

Internationally acclaimed photographer Roloff Beny saw his book, *To Every Thing There Is a Season* – a loving tribute to Canada – become a best seller. A book about the fortress of Louisbourg and another Canadian book called *The Trail of the Iroquois* had the same good luck. Canadiana sections of libraries had a hard time keeping up with demand.

Artists painted thousands of murals on Canadian themes; hundreds of new statues of Canadian heroes were unveiled in parks across the land. There were centennial teach-ins and centennial cookbooks. A bathtub race that was held in British Columbia has since become an annual event. A balloon race was held on the prairies. Festivals of all kinds abounded – potato festivals, tomato festivals, cherry festivals, and many more. The first bilingual drama festival was held in Moncton, New Brunswick, and the Dominion Drama Festival had the biggest crowds in its history.

The venerable Highland Games in Nova Scotia changed its name that year to the Nova Scotia Centennial Folk Arts Festival and Highland Games. John Fisher was there in a kilt to greet Sir Fitzroy MacLean of Scotland who said he had never felt more at home.

Other people started collecting old things. For Don MacKenzie of Ottawa it was old bottles – ten thousand of them – until, when there was no more room in his house for living or storage, he opened up the Bytown

The CBC put its staff and resources wholeheartedly into reporting the centennial celebrations. Bill McNeil (the author) was producer of a nightly radio program that followed events across the country and kept him in constant contact with Fisher throughout Centennial Year. Here, in a publicity photograph, McNeil (on the right), in his role as navigator of "Centennial Diary", strikes a nautical pose. On the left is Alan Maitland, "Centennial Diary" host, and oarsman of the CBC's entry in the first Vancouver bathtub race.

Fisher was an honorary chief
of seven Indian tribes in
Canada. Here Chief One Spot
Fisher takes part in a tree-
planting ceremony on the
Blood Indian reserve in
Alberta.

Bottle and Glass Museum. For Percy Bridges of New
Brunswick it was cow bells. One Yukon resident filled
every nook and cranny of his house with old telephones.

The owner of a dry-cleaning business offered to clean
Canadian or centennial flags "absolutely free of charge".
His "Fly a Clean Flag" campaign took off across the
country.

There were numerous events and accomplishments of
a more serious kind. There was an athletic awards
program for all Canadian schoolchildren. The Royal
Bank of Canada awarded a fifty-thousand-dollar
centennial prize to brain surgeon Wilder Penfield of
Montreal. An interfaith religious conference was held. A
youth travel program set up exchanges of groups of
youngsters all over the country. The influence of these
and other achievements – like the Canada Games, which
were started that year – are still felt today.

Canada's Native People had long protested that they
had insufficient guarantees of their rights, particularly in
relation to their ownership of land. Their champion
emerged in 1967 when Dr. Howard Adams announced
his intention to lead his people's fight and appeal for

justice to the Queen, in Britain. Native People across the country applauded the move. They also joined whole-heartedly in the centennial celebrations. Many travelled from the Yukon to Expo and shook hands with Prime Minister Pearson, and with John Fisher, who was an honorary chief of seven tribes. The Native Peoples' pavilion at Expo was one of the most popular exhibits. Also, a converted bus full of artifacts and historical materials was driven by Chief Jimmy Kitpoo from Halifax to Vancouver. The "Rolling Reserve" was visited by thousands of people wherever it stopped along the way.

It was a great year for Canadians, many of whom were travelling and seeing their country for the first time. One lucky group of schoolchildren took the centennial abroad, to Mount Kilimanjaro in Tanzania. There the children triumphantly planted the Canadian flag on the mountain's summit.

The American state of Alaska was celebrating its centennial, too, and joint events were arranged on both sides of the border. All over Canada, international events enhanced the national festivities. Canada hosted an International Air Show, an International Soccer Match, and a World Congress of Police Officers.

A helicopter took off from the fortress of Louisbourg in Cape Breton and, for the next hundred days, flew in a westerly direction towards its final stop in Vancouver. It was the first time such a long trip had been undertaken in a helicopter. In the Yukon the first stagecoach-to-helicopter mail pickup was made.

Many people, including Hank the centennial walker, walked across Canada. The Trans-Canada Highway was crowded with cross-country travellers, centennial hitch-hikers, walkers who wouldn't accept rides, drivers in ancient cars, and others in all forms of vehicles. One man made the trip on a donkey. Another travelled by oxcart. Still another made the distance in a snowmobile. Students from Simon Fraser University rode across the continent in a hearse and declared it "the only way to go". A senior citizen rode his bike the whole 4000 miles, while Philip Moane and his dog, Bruno, walked together from Halifax to Vancouver.

Centennial Commissioner John Fisher was probably the busiest traveller of all. He criss-crossed the country more than a hundred times that year. In four years of centennial campaigning, he had travelled almost half a million kilometres. He added another quarter of a million during the big year itself.

It was fun and games and a bag full of pride for twelve glorious months. John Fisher's enjoyment of the celebrations was plain to see. He had a right to be proud. He more than anyone else was responsible for the success of the centennial.

If John Fisher did nothing else in his lifetime, his creation of Centennial Year would have been enough to earn him the title "Mr. Canada". For the millions who visited Canada during 1967, John Fisher's friendly face was the face of Canada. It was his face they saw wherever they travelled. He lent his presence to every- thing that happened. He opened fairs, christened buildings, and welcomed the potentates of the world.

His warm enthusiastic voice could be heard every- where, urging Canadians to "live it up and cast off those drab grey tones of mediocrity." "You're the best in the world," he proclaimed, "and it's time the world should know." As he kept up his endless travels his presence in a community could create great excitement. He often outshone the celebrities he was there to introduce.

The year 1967 was not just Canada's year, it was John Fisher's year, too. With it he climaxed a lifetime of selling Canada to the world and to Canadians themselves. He was only fifty-five years old when the centennial celebrations ended, but for "Mr. Canada", his life's dream had been realized. More important, although Centennial Year might be over, out of its experiences had come a new sense of unity and nationalism for Canadians. John Fisher had helped to give Canada the best possible start on its second century of nationhood.

The Final Years Chapter 8

Centennial Year was a great accomplishment, both for John Fisher and for the country he loved. In fact, it had been so spectacular that it was difficult even for a man like John Fisher to move on to greater achievements.

In October 1967, when Centennial Year was almost over, Fisher resigned his post as Centennial Commissioner. He could safely do so, confident in the knowledge that the celebrations had been a triumphant success.

Fisher's reward for the superb job he had done was a simple one. He could take pleasure and pride in what had been accomplished for Canadian nationalism during 1967. At one time, there had been talk of a more concrete reward. When Prime Minister John Diefenbaker had appointed Fisher to the post of Centennial Commissioner, he had suggested that afterwards there might be a seat in the Senate for John Fisher.

The idea had appealed to Fisher. He had long felt that the frequently criticized upper house could be a much more important and useful part of the Canadian democracy if it were given a chance. He saw the Senate as the proper vehicle in which to continue the business of raising the national consciousness of Canadians.

It was not to be, however. The government had changed. The Liberals had come to power; the Conservatives were out. John Diefenbaker was no longer making the Senate appointments, and John Fisher was allowed to leave with little or no fanfare.

Fisher did a number of things afterwards, including running a newspaper chain and his own public relations firm, John Fisher Enterprises. Also he was much in demand as an adviser to groups running centennial or other kinds of anniversary celebrations. When the Province of Manitoba was planning its centennial for the year 1970, John Fisher accepted an invitation to act as consultant. As in the larger celebration of 1967, citizens of the province pitched in with great zeal. There were once again the individual centennial projects and the

After Fisher's departure from the Centennial Commission, there were many lunches and dinners from grateful friends.

John Fisher with his second wife, Cathy, on holiday in the Canadian Rockies. The couple were married in 1974.

larger public projects, some of which have great importance today. Two examples are the non-profit natural history museum, the Manitoba Museum of Man and Nature, and the Manitoba Theatre Centre, the first major regional theatre in Canada. The MTC had been founded in 1958, but in 1970, as a centennial project, it moved into its own building – a 786-seat theatre.

After this, at the invitation of the Government of the United States, Fisher became an adviser to groups planning the American bicentennial celebrations of 1976. Very few people in the world could claim to be "centennial experts". Fisher certainly was one, and so his services were much in demand.

Although he enjoyed this kind of work, Fisher had always loved broadcasting, and now he longed to get back into it. People were urging him to use his talents in radio again. In 1970, when Fisher's work on the Manitoba centennial was finished, Bill McNeil (the author) called Fisher at his office in Toronto and asked him if he'd be willing to revive "John Fisher Reports" for a CBC radio series called "Assignment". Fisher jumped at the opportunity and said that he had thought of suggesting the same idea himself. He was concerned that there had been an apparent falling off of Canadian nationalism in the three years since the centennial, and said he'd be willing to give the new program a try.

Once again the Fisher voice was heard on the Canadian airwaves, and once again the magic began to work. Listeners wrote from all over the country, welcoming him back. In 1971, when "Assignment" ended, Bill McNeil persuaded Fisher to join him on a new program called "Fresh Air". These broadcasts were to be heard in Ontario and Quebec only. Once again, Fisher's Sunday morning broadcasts built up a large following.

From then until 1978 Fisher came in regularly to the studio for his broadcast. It was always a pleasure for his old friends at the CBC to see his ruddy, smiling face and hefty form, and to talk to the man who was never without a good story.

Those who saw him on a weekly basis, were slow to notice that he was losing weight. At last, however, the changes in his appearance began to be noticeable. Suddenly, hefty John was not just thin, he was skinny!

When McNeil asked John one day if he was on a diet, Fisher quietly broke the bad news. He had cancer. But, he was quick to add, he was going to fight it. He then asked permission to record his broadcasts three or four at a time so that he could travel to some of the world's best cancer clinics. Art Crighton, the producer of "Fresh Air", quickly agreed, and Mr. Canada set out over the next three years in search of a cure.

John travelled to Europe, to Mexico, to New York. He went just about any place where a ray of hope was offered. He began carrying his portable tape recorder with him to record his weekly broadcasts. Whenever he returned to Toronto, he was smaller and thinner, but not beaten. When he was away he sent post cards saying things like: "I'm going to wrestle this thing to the ground."

On November 29, 1980 – John Fisher's sixty-seventh birthday – his wife, Cathy, his son, John, and two of his oldest friends, Lou Cahill and Bill McNeil, gathered in his room at the Wellesley Hospital in Toronto for a small party, complete with cake and candles. The guests sang "Happy Birthday", and John's eyes glistened with tears as he said, simply, "Thank you, my friends." Those were the only words he spoke that day.

Fisher makes a point. Although he didn't reduce the lectern to kindling wood like his maternal grandfather, John Fisher was a forceful speaker.

Shortly afterwards, Mrs. Fisher took John to Florida for the winter, so that he could enjoy the warmth of the sun. There were to be "no more clinics and no more cures". John Fisher died there on February 15, 1981. His remains lie in the family plot in Mount Pleasant cemetery in Toronto.

To those who knew him well, John Fisher was a "darlin' man". Extremely generous, his friends' only worry was that he would give away everything he had. Generous is the word that probably fitted him best. He was giving of himself and of the talents that were bestowed on him as well.

To all those who marvelled at him over the years he was what he appeared to be – a great Canadian. His life was dedicated to one purpose – that of making his countrymen more aware of the potential of the land they lived in, and making other countries of the world more aware of Canada.

Further Reading

Fisher, John. *The Complete Cross-Canada Quiz and Game Book*. Toronto: McClelland and Stewart Limited, 1978.

———. *John Fisher Reports: An Anthology of Radio Scripts*. Hamilton, Ontario: Niagara Editorial Bureau, 1949.

Karsh, Yousuf and John Fisher. *Yousuf Karsh & John Fisher See Canada*. Toronto: Thomas Allen Limited, 1960.

McNeil, Bill and Morris Wolfe. *Signing On: The Birth of Radio in Canada*. Toronto: Doubleday Canada Limited, 1982.

Credits and Acknowledgments

Every effort has been made to credit all sources correctly. The author and publishers will welcome any information that will allow them to correct any errors or omissions.

The publishers wish to express their gratitude to the following who have given permission to use copyright illustrations in this book:
E.A. Ballinger (Public Archives of Nova Scotia), pages 15, 30
Canadian Broadcasting Corporation, pages 19, 20, 47, 57
Canadian Broadcasting Corporation, French-language section, page 53
Cathy Fisher, pages 13, 14, 38, 46, 61, 62, cover
George Fisher, pages 3, 7, 9, 10, 11, 16, 17, 23, 38
Fisher family, Sackville, New Brunswick, page 8
The Globe and Mail, page 54
Lloyd Knight, *Lethbridge Herald*, page 58
Bill McNeil, pages 53, 56
Hugh Mills, page 26
Robert Norwood (Public Archives of Nova Scotia), page 27
Ontario Editorial Bureau, title page, pages 33, 39, 40, 43, 48, 55
Ontario Provincial Archives, pages 36, 42, 44, 50, 63
Public Archives of Nova Scotia, page 28
Strathey Smith, page 48
Lloyd E. Thompson, page 51
United Press International, page 49
Margaret (Vollmer) Whitmore, pages 31, 32, 34

The author wishes to thank the following for their help and co-operation:
The Canadian Broadcasting Corporation/Radio Canada
Cathy Fisher
John Fisher, Jr.
Ned Fisher
John Grimshaw
James Kerr
Pamela Lewis
Eileen McNeil

Index

Aird Commission, 19, 21

Bennett, R.B. (Prime Minister), 12, 21, 43

Cahill, Lou, 39-40, 63
Canadian Broadcasting Corporation (CBC), 5, 18-22, 23, 31, 32, 38, 57, 62-63
Canadian Tourist Association (CTA), 42
Centennial Canoe Pageant, 55-56
Centennial Commission, 45-48
Centennial Train, 54-55
Centennial Year, 49-60
CHNS radio, 16, 17, 22, 24, 27

Dalhousie Law School/University, 15, 22, 23
Depression, The, 11-12, 14-15, 21
Diefenbaker, John (Prime Minister), 42-45, 61

Expo '67, 53

Fisher, Audrey, 38
Fisher, Cathy, 62-63
Fisher, Frederick Arnold, 3, 7, 10
Fisher, John, Jr., 38
Fisher, Norah Wiggins, 3, 7
Frosty Hollow, N.B., 3, 8-12, 23

Gimby, Bobby, 57

Halifax, N.S., 15-17, 22-29

"John Fisher Reports", 6, 31-41

LaMarsh, Judy, 48, 49
Louisbourg, N.S., 24-25

Mackenzie King, William Lyon (Prime Minister), 19, 21
McGuinness, Fred, 46
Mills, Hugh ("Uncle Mel"), 16, 22, 26, 29, 30, 45
Mount Allison University, 8, 14

Pearson, Lester B. (Prime Minister), 50, 58-59

Queen Elizabeth II, 49-50, 53, 54

Roberts, Sir Charles G.D., 40
Rothesay Collegiate, 9, 13, 14

Sackville, N.B., 8-12
Second World War, 26-30, 35, 37
Stanfield, Robert, 15, 16

Vollmer, Margaret, 31, 32

"Westinghouse Presents", 32-33
Wiggins, Dr. Cecil, 9, 63
Willis, J. Frank, 22